The Flying "Z" Ranch

The Life of Ron Ziegler

Ron Ziegler

ISBN: 978-1-62269-036-7

Who Will Tell Your Stories To The Next Generation?

Write Heart Memories®

Ultimate Workbooks, Published Stories & Interviews With Beth Lord
Preserving Legacy & You In A Book

206-929-0024 | www.bethlord.com | beth@bethlord.com

DEDICATION

This book is dedicated to my father, Ray Ziegler and to my uncle, Allen Ziegler. Thanks for the many things you both taught me over the years. Yes, I know I was not the greatest student. However, over the years I did manage to learn a great many things from my two mentors. Thank you both for putting up with me. I am forever thankful to you both.

Love, Ron

Contents

A Little Story To Begin This Book

It's a beautiful day here. We have high clouds, but not very many and the sun is shining. It's probably going to be 70 to 75 degrees out today, and it's gorgeous. I'm going to take my two dogs out for a walk around the place, so they get a little exercise. I have a black lab who weighs about 90 pounds. And then I have a pit bull mix, weighs about 70 pounds. It is an interesting story about these two dogs. The older dog is the black lab who is about seven years old. He had gone into retirement - laying around sleeping, and not doing much all day. Then we brought home this new little puppy that was the pit bull mix and what a difference it made. The old dog came out of retirement and they play together. They are the best of friends, and I'm sure it has added two to three years to the black lab's life. And this explains why my wife, Betty, is interviewing for a new ranch manager.

Foreward

So my first thought is, "*Why am I writing this book? Well, I'm doing this because I'm 83 years old now. And I would hope that my grandchildren and my great-grandchildren will have something to look back on and know what their grandfather and great-grandfather was about.*"

I would love to have known more about my grandparents' lives. They were already older when I was young, thus I never had an opportunity to talk to them, and now there is nothing left for me to get to know them better. My grandparents on my father's side had been immigrants from Lithuania, and they married here. My grandparents from my mother's side came from Sweden. Thus, all my grandparents were immigrants to this country. And again, I'd love to know more about what their early lives were like when they were in Lithuania and Sweden. But that's not available to me. So hopefully, this will be a little idea that my grandkids can take a look at one of these days and get an idea of what it was like when I was growing up so I'm going to start there.

Chapter One
Growing Up In Hermosa Beach, California

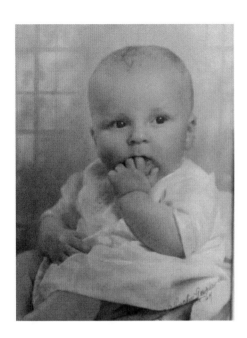 

I was born November 18, 1937 in Los Angeles. My parents were Ray and Esther and I was the first of five children born to them - myself, Ken, Douglas, Judi, and Tom.

Growing up we lived in a small little town out of Los Angeles near the ocean named Hermosa Beach. Our house was about five blocks from the ocean, and there was a beautiful beach there. My early childhood has fond memories of going to the beach and having a great time in the water. I loved surfing and fishing and Hermosa Beach was the perfect place.

There was a small grammar school nearby with a kindergarten through the sixth grade, called North School. North School was within walking distance of our family house. I'd walk to school starting in kindergarten through the sixth grade. After sixth grade, I went to junior high school. Junior high school was called Pier Avenue and were seventh and eighth grades. High school was named Mira Costa High School and was within walking distance although as soon as I turned 16, I had a car and drove. I graduated from high school when I was 17 and turned 18 that fall.

SCHOOL DAYS 1950-'51
Pier Ave.

I want my grandkids to know that I was fortunate and had a wonderful childhood in Hermosa Beach. Now Hermosa Beach is crowded and congested, but when I was a kid, there were still lots of vacant lots. My neighbors had horses, and we'd go riding all day and would be gone until we had to come back for dinner. We were on our own, and that was a great feeling. The times were safer than today.

It was the best time for fun and creativity. We could go in the street in front of our house and play hit the bat, hide and seek, and all kinds of other games. It was a wonderful time to grow up. I wouldn't trade that time for anything. I think the kids of today who are indoors watching television all day or playing video games, are missing a childhood.

My first car was a 1946 Ford convertible that my Uncle Al had given me, probably around 1952. It wasn't old, but for automobiles in those days, if your car went one hundred thousand miles, you were the king of the road. Nobody did better than one hundred thousand miles on a vehicle. Today, cars last much longer. We used to go around from house to house and collect bottles because bottles had a deposit. The small coke bottle or small soda bottle had a two-cent deposit on it. So, if we could collect 50 of those bottles, we had a dollar. And if we had a dollar, then we had enough money to take the car, go to the gas station and buy about three gallons of gasoline. Gasoline was 15 or 18 cents a gallon. So, for about 45 cents, we could put three gallons of gas in the car. There was a local hamburger place called Clancy's Hamburgers, and you could get a Clancy's hamburger for about fifteen cents with a Coke and some

French fries. Then we would go to the show. Now, that seems fantastic, but that's absolutely the way it was and what you could get for a dollar.

Senior High School Picture

After I graduated from Mira Costa high school in 1955, I went to Ventura College for a couple of years. I was short of credits, and went to USC in Los Angeles for a short time, but did not graduate. I am sorry about that, and if there was one thing I could have done differently, I would have graduated from college. Something I should have done.

At the time, I was a terrible student, and received bad grades. I thought I was a bad student because I was not very smart. Later on, as I became older, I found that if I wanted to apply myself, sit down and spend some time on the material, I can learn most whatever I need to learn, and I'm able to pass the tests and get it done. But in my younger years, I didn't think was the case. It's something that has occurred to me later in life.

I guess you could say maturity comes with age.

If I had to do it over again as a young person, I should have joined the military. Looking back, I was immature. Had I gone into the military for a couple of years, that would have given me a little chance to mature, and I would have done better in school.

I found this old 1937 Ford panel truck in an auto junkyard. No engine or transmission. In the same junkyard, I found a Ford V-8 and 3-speed transmission. We towed the truck home to my Mom's driveway. She and my Dad were not too happy with my find. The truck had been painted a gold color and was missing a back fender. My friends and I were able to reinstall the engine and transmission and get the truck running. In those days, I was a surfer. Any surfer of standing had a panel truck with a mattress and surfboard in the back of the truck. I had a great time driving to the beach, getting my surfboard out, and enjoying the surf. After doing this for several months, my lifelong friend Terry Huff and I started planning a fishing and surfing exploration trip to Baja, California, across Mexico's border. Terry and I made the trip. About 300 miles below the Mexican border and back without breaking down or getting stopped by the American highway patrol or the Mexican price. In Mexico, we discovered a dry salt flat used to test fast cars to see just how fast they would go. Terry and I decided to make a speed run in the '39 Ford truck. We made it about 200 feet until the salt turned to mud. Some local fisherman rescued us by pushing us out of the mud. After this, we jointly decided to cut the adventure short and go home.

Chapter Two
My Work Ethic

I was on my way to becoming a surfer when one Saturday morning when I was about 12 years old, sleeping, my father came into my bedroom and said, "*Ron, get up. You're going to go to work with me today.*" And I said, "*No, Dad. It's Saturday, and I'm going to the beach today. And besides, I am still sleeping so I won't be getting up and I won't be going to work with you.*" He said, *If you don't get up and get out of bed right now, I'm going to go get a glass of cold water, pull the sheets off of you and throw the water on you while you're in your bed.*" I didn't get out of bed, and he did get the glass of water, and threw it on me. I was all wet, and so, of course, I had to get out of bed and get going. I went to see his business, and after that, I started going with Dad down to his business regularly.

It worked out okay because I was not a very good surfer anyway. My Dad would give me a thirty-minute verbal sales meeting coming and going in the car when I went to work with him. I didn't know how much I was learning from these talks but they came in very handy as I grew up.

The family business was originally called West Coast Supply, later abbreviated to Westco Products, and the basis of the company was taking bakery ingredients like flour, sugar, raisins, and walnuts and reselling them to people in the bakery, candy, and confection business.

It had been started by my grandfather (John) and his three sons - Ray, Paul and Allen. After a short period of time, Paul, who was the eldest brother, left the business. My grandfather passed away and that left my Dad and Al in charge, and they owned it. It was located at 1654 Long Beach Avenue in Los Angeles. It was a small warehouse near downtown Los Angeles.

My growing up years were the ending of the War years, gasoline was 15, 16 cents a gallon. You had to have ration cards to purchase anything so it was difficult to get any sugar, eggs or gasoline. The idea of not being able to get sugar in the bakery business created tremendous problems.

Sugar was unavailable. In our company's case, we had an allotment because we were in business before the war and that meant whatever you had been using, say 1000 bags a year, you were allowed that amount but nothing more. There were orders not to sell the sugar for more than what you had sold it for before the war. The government was trying to stop profiteering by increasing the price of the sugar due to the shortage of sugar. If you were a baker and you needed sugar, you would pay whatever to purchase a bag.

Because of our allotment, the company began to think about making the sugar into something else so they began to make a simple raspberry jelly. I remember them making the jelly. There was a large copper kettle filled to the top with water, sugar, pectin, artificial flavor, and colors. It was then placed on a candy stove and cooked into a syrup. The candy stove had a large gas burner in it and concentric rings on the top of the stove and you would take those rings out depending upon the cooking area you wanted to have. The syrup was poured into 40-pound steel cans, and that was a pail of jelly. Some acid was added to it, which would make the jelly setup. When it cooled off, it was ready for sale. One batch might be three pails of jelly, so it was a small operation. The jelly was the beginning of our manufacturing process, and it started around 1942-1944.

I started working there on Saturdays, school holidays, and summers. I started out sweeping the floor or doing whatever needed doing and this was my introduction to working. I found out after a little while that I enjoyed it. There were several of the other employees that I was friends with, and if everything worked out well and I was there at the right time, I could go out with one of the drivers on one of the trucks and make deliveries. This activity was fun because the bakers and candy people that we were delivering to would give me free donuts and cookies. So, I had plenty of sweets to eat. One of the drivers I would often go with was a man by the name of Daniel Valles. We got to be good friends, and he was one of my mentors in life.

I think everybody has different people who are important to them in their development because they teach you things. Daniel taught me a lot about how to work and why to work. So later on, as the business grew, Daniel became the warehouse manager. When he was warehouse manager, I used to work directly for him. One of the most important things he taught me was to grab a broom and start sweeping if you have nothing to do. Don't just stand there and do nothing, do something.

He also taught me a lot about mechanical things. We had an old welding machine, and he was there to teach me how to work on my car. Then I was able to find enough time to fool around with that welding machine and further teach myself how to weld. This has been a very valuable skill for me for my whole life. I live on a ranch now, and there always seems to be something broken around that needs repairing, and I'm able to do that because Daniel had been there to teach me. I can't talk about the company without talking a little bit about my other mentors, who were my Uncle, Al Ziegler. He was an intelligent guy and taught me a tremendous amount. My Dad was also a very intelligent man, and he also taught me a tremendous amount. So between my Dad and my Uncle, I had a tremendous education and their advice was invaluable in my learning in business.

As the company grew, so did our prepared fruit filling. A batch size went from a couple hundred pounds to 2500 pounds, so the batches became considerably more significant. The machinery became better, and larger portions were automated. We also made many flour mixes where the flour was blended with salt, sugar, shortening, flavors, and colors, producing various prepared mixes. So, if you had a donut shop and you wanted to make a raised donut, we could and would make a raised donut mix for you. If you wanted a cake donut mix, we could make a cake donut mix. If a bakery contacted us and requested a blend for Danish, we could make those mixes as well. Originally, the mixes were all packed in 100-pound bags. Later, the industry changed from one hundred-pound bags to 50-pound bags. And a batch of that mix was, I think, twenty-five hundred pounds. So, that would have meant there were 50 - 50-pound bags in one quantity. One of our better mixes was the Buttermilk cruller mix.

The first branch we had was located in Phoenix and it was quite small. Then a branch was opened in Salt Lake City, another in the San

Francisco Bay Area. Eventually we had 10 branches. There were also branches in Reno, Las Vegas, Sacramento, Portland, OR and Seattle, WA.

Reflecting, I think we were a fair manufacturer. When it came to marketing and selling goods, we were far better than the competition. That was credit to my Dad and my Uncle. They both understood business. In the early days, my brother, Ken also was a salesman for the company, and eventually became branch manager in Union City - near San Francisco. Ken did not like living in that area so he moved back to Los Angeles. My Uncle Al and Kenny's personalities were not compatible. They were like gasoline and fire together, and always creating explosions. Kenny left the company and started his own real estate development company and has done very well.

Early on, when I was going to school and working at West Coast Supply, my Dad came to me one day and said, *"You know, Ron; we have an opportunity that you might be interested in San Diego. One of our salesmen there has quit. And we have that San Diego territory open. If you'd like to think about being a salesman, you can go to San Diego and take that small territory."* There were only enough customers there for about two days, every other week of work. Of course, I said, *"Sure, I would do that."* I started going to San Diego. The story of San Diego is like this: we had at that time a full-time salesman in San Diego, whose name was Sam Gerard. Sam had a son whose name was Bob, and Bob had a small territory. What Sam had done was he had split the area up and kept the better accounts for himself and gave the less desirable, more troubled accounts to his son. Bob had done this for a couple of years and didn't care to do it anymore. So, he left. That became my opportunity to have a few customers. I was 19.

So there I was, 19 years old, calling on customers who were twice or three times my age, but I got along with them, and the territory slowly grew. I must have done a reasonable job because I was offered another territory when it became available, and of course I took it. I was calling on customers in the Oxnard area and then driving north along the Central Coast to Paso Robles. Thus, this became another territory with new customers. One week I went to San Diego, and then the next week I drove from Oxnard to Paso Robles, where I was making calls to donut shops and bakeries. If the donut shop or bakery was buying ingredients, we were trying to sell them. Schools, colleges, and supermarkets were all our potential customers. In those days, very few supermarkets had any bakeries in them. That was a trend that came much later.

I did that for three or four years. In the meantime, I married Betty when we were 21. At the time, we were close to the last of our group to marry. Most everyone our age was already married. It was 1958, and kids got married earlier than now. It was a different time. The young people these days are taking longer to get established and take on responsibility.

Our company had always sold some bakery equipment. If someone needed an oven or showcases, we were there to sell them what they needed. Later, we had an official department for bakery equipment, I was in charge of that division.

I then started working in Los Angeles every day, and the job entailed selling the bakery equipment, drawing the plans for where the showcases would go, getting them delivered, and installing them. At that time, our company sold a tremendous amount of bakery and donut showcases. We were the dealer for a company out of Columbus, Ohio, called Columbus Showcase Company. The showcases would come from Columbus in big, railcars. There would be 50, 60, or 70 bakery display cases in each railcar, stacked up inside the railcar, two and three high. We would unload them from the railcar and put them into our warehouse and then sell them, take from our warehouse, deliver, and install. So that became my job for a while.

The next thing that happened is that the company had six or seven salesmen, and the sales manager's name was Leo Zweig. Leo was always at odds with the salesmen and customers and eventually parted ways. Dad came to me and said he wanted me to be the sales manager. So at 26 years old I became the sales manager and it seemed relatively easy because if I developed a problem that I didn't know how to deal with or handle, I simply went to my Dad and asked him what to do, he would tell me and that was the end of the problem. Well, I had been doing that for maybe two years when suddenly my Dad passed away at the age of 56 from a heart attack, and I had to be on my own. I had to muddle through for a few years, but my Dad, Ray, was very experienced in sales and marketing, and I had learned from that exposure.

My youngest brother, Tom, was still in high school when Dad passed away and he never went into the business. He moved to Idaho and became a successful building contractor. My sister, Judi, was in college. She graduated and married a man who became a pilot for Western Airlines, which eventually became Delta Airlines.

My area was sales and marketing. Maybe that's why I think we did it better than anybody else. At that time the salesmen were paid a commission - around 5% of gross sales, based on different products -flavors was 11%, flour shortening was 1%. The more you sold, the more you made. Salesmen paid for everything themselves - automobiles, gas etc. I learned what happens when customers say no, and what you can do to turn that around. It was a great learning time for me. For example, with MacMix, I learned that if you make a large batch at the beginning of the week and put it in a pastry bag then you can take it out when you need more macaroon cookies and bake them. The fact that you can put it away in the refrigerator and keep it for a week was a big selling point. My brother, Douglas, invented MacMix.

Salesmen are scared to death in collecting the money. The time to bring money up is when you begin the relationship, and tell the customer what you expect from them and what you want them to do. In return, you will take care of them and their needs. There's an agreement from the very beginning with the first order, the next time you come into that store, the customer will pay you. Uncle Al was the one who enforced the collection policies and I learned a lot from him.

Everyone serves in an apprenticeship no matter what your trade is.

Don't prejudge the sale because you don't know what that person is going to order. And don't be afraid to ask for the order. Be sensitive to what the customer is saying to you. I don't think anyone can stand behind you and teach you this listening skill. You can't learn it from a class either. You learn from making face to face sales calls.

Warren Bradley was in charge of the factory in those days and he was a difficult guy even though he was brilliant. We had a teamster union in the factory, and the company had been negotiating with the teamster membership for a new contract. Warren had done this on his own for years but for some reason, we kept him out of the negotiations. The teamsters liked the contract and so did the employees but Warren told the employees to turn it down and they did. It was a 100% failure vote on the contract, even the team who had organized this contract voted against it. The factory was 100% black and so was Bradley. The next day after it was voted down, Bradley said to the employees to not do anything productive. It was management, organizing a strike.

When my Uncle heard about this, he told Bradley to tell the employees to go back to work. Bradley said he would not. This is an important point because in Labor Law an employee cannot refuse a direct order unless it's illegal, dangerous or something along those lines. Bradley was discharged and fired. When the employees went home and came back the next day, guess what? All the formulas for the entire factory were gone. All the files had been cleaned out. Not a formula left. The jelly, the jams and the filling and the donut mixes were all gone. We had thought something like this might happen so about a month before, my brother, Douglas had photocopied all of the formulas and had taken them home with him. So, he went home, retrieved the formulas, brought them back and production resumed. We were back in business.

Formulas change over time as formulas are adjusted. Fortunately for us, the people who were doing the manufacturing for us remembered what the adjustments were. We didn't miss a beat. It was interesting to see how supportive the employees were of management because most of them understood what was going on. Bradley was playing the race card for his own purposes.

Bradley sued the company for termination. He said he hadn't done anything wrong and he was dismissed because he was black and his being 56 - age discrimination. This was 1975 and the LA jury was 90% black. We lost the case. The damages were for $70,000.00 but Bradley had sued for a million and a half dollars. We were offered another trial, but when we had an opportunity to talk to the jury members, we decided otherwise. This jury didn't believe our witnesses even though they were our employees. If we went to trial again and the jury found us guilty, the damages could have been more. We settled it there.

After Bradley left the company, Douglas became in charge of the factory and manufacturing. He stepped in and reorganized the factory. He improved the sanitation issues and moved the factory to a new location. It was in an old industrial location. We started with two buildings each on 20x100-foot lots. As we needed more space so we purchased another lot and then another until our buildings constituted almost a full city block.

Across the street was a rail spur we used for our parking lot for our employees and to unload an occasional railcar. One day the railway company came along and said, *"Guess What? We're taking away the rail spur and you're going to lose your parking lot. We have plans to turn it into a blue line rail system from LA to Long Beach"* This was a major concern for the business. It was forcing us to relocate our office and manufacturing. If Doug had not been in charge of the factory, it would have been difficult to move. We found another location in Pico Riviera that had been a food plant and we were able to buy that location and relocate.

When I reflect back, this was a piece of monumental luck for us because it forced us into a new plant. And I do mean forced because none of us wanted to move. The new plant solved a lot of problems, like always being one step ahead of the health department. We had severe rodent problems. We were able to keep growing after we moved into the new facility. The business was in a perfect position because we were in an industry that was growing. We were getting more and more shares of the market all the time. We were developing branch locations that had a warehouse, factories, salesmen, truck drivers, and people in various places.

We ended up with ten different branches around the western part of the United States. We had a manufacturing plant in Seattle, San Francisco Bay Area, Salt Lake City, and the main plant in Los Angeles. In addition to that, we had branch warehouses where we would sell the merchandise and deliver it in Portland, Sacramento, Reno, Phoenix, and of course, Los Angeles. I think at one time we had a total of 10 different branches and they're still there and operating, as far as I know. We went from six salespeople to approximately 70 when I retired. The company was sold in 1991, and since then, there are hundreds of salesmen. So, the company has continued to grow and has become considerably more significant. The new owners renamed Westco "Bakemark". You often see their trucks up and down the freeways delivering merchandise to customers.

Something I have thought a lot about were the Westco employees. Over the years with 10 plus locations up and down the West Coast we never had a call telling us a branch had not opened for business that day. People get sick and occurrences happen. This never stopped our business from day to day…. trucks were loaded, goods were delivered, invoices were printed…. our system worked, thanks to our employees. The majority of our employees were with us their entire career. We had any number who were there 30 to 40 years. They are the ones who took care of the company and customers. Westco was fortunate to have people who cared about the company and did what was necessary to keep everything running…. we never received a call that a branch had not opened or a Westco truck had not delivered the merchandise. I give a big thank you to the office people, the warehouse men, truck drivers, and of course the sales staff…who all made it happen. A very big piece of Westco's success came directly from the employees.

Part of what happened to us in the early days was, the company only owned the real estate in Los Angeles and rented warehouses in the other locations. Around 1970, (my Dad had already passed away), I went to my Uncle, and I said *"Listen, Al, it's crazy that we rent these buildings. Why don't we buy them and own them ourselves?"* He wasn't too much of a real estate guy, and was negative to the idea. I said to him "*Look, if you don't want to do it, let me do it by myself. I'll build a building and rent it back to the company.*" My first building was in Beaverton, Oregon.

I found a contractor and an empty lot in Beaverton, Oregon. Back then there wasn't much in Beaverton. In 1970, it was bleak - unspoiled and rural. We found a one-acre piece of property. Generally speaking, if you buy one acre which has forty-three thousand feet in it, you can usually occupy a building that's 50 percent of the location space you have. We could build a twenty-thousand-foot building. I think we built an eighteen thousand five hundred square foot warehouse building. The company moved from a rental building in Portland to the new building in Beaverton. That was my introduction to the real estate business. And since then, I've had a fortunate career in purchasing and leasing warehouse buildings.

As this became a successful idea, the company decided it was a good idea. My uncle, my brother, and I began buying buildings and renting them back to the company. It worked out well. But in addition to that, I was able to find some buildings on my own, which I was able to purchase, so now Betty and I have several warehouse buildings around California that we rent to various tenants, not the company. They've been terrific real estate. They've been much better than I ever would have imagined. I wish I could tell you that I had a grand plan about how this was going to work, but I didn't. It happened by chance. The real estate values were going up, and you could just about pick out any piece of ground you wanted to pick out, and it was going to go up in value. I was looking at a lease this morning for a property that's here in the town of Santa Maria near our ranch. The contract is dated 2003. So that means I've had that building for fifteen years already. Fifteen years went by very, very fast.

The rents have gone up. The values have gone up. And so what started to be just kind of a mediocre investment has turned out to be an excellent investment. That's pretty much the case on all of our real estate ventures. It's always the same story. If I think about the advice that I would like to leave my son, my grandkids and my great-grandkids, I would say, "*Try to buy things that go up in value.* "

Real estate is a prime example. If you buy it today, probably tomorrow, it's going to be worth more money. Indeed, in ten years, it will be worth more money. Inflation, in that respect is your friend because you buy it with dollars that have today's value. But in ten years, the dollars are going to be inflated, and you're going to be paying them off with cheaper dollars. And try to stay away from things that go down in value, especially new fancy, expensive cars that as soon as you drive them off the showroom floor, they lose 20 or 30 percent of their value.

I remember my Dad liking to play the Monopoly game. It taught you that having a piccc of propcrty docsn't do anything for you, but putting something on it does. You put something on the property and then somebody pays you rent for it. Then you do much better. The longer you have it, the more rent you get. The building in Beaverton is a good example. When we started renting that building, it was eighteen cents a foot. And today, the same rental on that building is probably sixty-five cents a foot. So, it just gives you an idea of how the rental income has gone up, up and up. We sold the building some time ago and replaced it with another building, but it just gives you an idea about how things increase in value.

The other beautiful thing about warehouse buildings is generally there is only one tenant. You don't have very many problems with the building, as opposed to an apartment where you have multiple tenants and multiple issues. I prefer warehouse buildings, and I would recommend to my grandkids and my son they continue to do this. It has worked very well for Betty and myself.

Chapter Three
Family

When I was 19, I started dating my wife *"to be"* Betty. We went together for a couple of years, and by the time we were 21, we decided to get married. I asked her if she would marry me and she said she would. We were married on December the 6th, nineteen fifty-eight, which is over 60 years ago. And as I look back on it, it's one of the best decisions I ever made in that we have had a wonderful life together.

When you're 21 years old, you think that you have everything figured out, but you don't. The fact that I was able to figure out that Betty was the person to marry me was mostly good luck. I've always been happy I had enough smarts to figure that out. But again, it was a matter of luck, more than brains. And it's been a lot of fun and a great time. I'm pleased about that.

Married December 6, 1958

I want to talk a little bit about our children. We had two sons. The oldest one's name is Tim. And Tim has three children, our grandkids. They are Tommy, Megan, and Rachael. They all graduated from college and are on to their own adventures in life. Unfortunately, our younger son Jeff was injured in an accident when he was 21. He fell off of a cliff and sustained traumatic brain injury as a result of the fall. He had a disability for the rest of his rather short life. He never gained his equilibrium back and suffered complications of the brain injury until he died about 20 years after the accident.

I would like to talk a little more about our son, Tim. Tim, like myself, started working for the company in the warehouse when he was in his teens. He loaded trucks, helped with deliveries, and when necessary, swept the floors. Similar to myself, he was able to become a salesman while very young. Tim excels in fishing, motorcycle riding and mountain biking. He learned the fishing and motorcycle riding from his father. What I should have been teaching him was what the inside of a college looked like but it had never interested me, either. Baja, California and the ocean were much more of interest and exciting. So that is how Tim grew up. Most people who have been reading this story will not realize that when a family owned company is sold to new owners, the original family members still employed will soon be gone. This is almost a 100% rule. You can look at any family business within five years after being sold there will be no family members still employed. It is a great pride that our son Tim is still working for the company. The company was sold around 28 years ago and under a third new owner. Tim is one of few remaining original employees and still has one of the best sales territories. So, I guess teaching him about motorcycles and fishing turned out ok. He is a great salesman and we get fresh fish on occasion. Betty and I are extremely proud of our son Tim. I only wish I was as good a fisherman, motorcycle rider and salesman as he is.

Chapter Four
The Flying "Z" Ranch

When I was a salesman, part of my territory was what's called the north coast area around Solvang and the Santa Ynez Valley. In Solvang, I had an excellent customer, Birkholm's Bakery, going back to 1956. I remember thinking how beautiful this area was but never, ever dreamt that I might one day live here. About four or five years before we sold the business and I retired, Betty and I started looking for a place to have a vacation house or a place to get out of the city for the weekends. We started looking for five acres, but couldn't find anything because, generally, the properties were larger. So, we looked for 20 acres and there was nothing, so we ended up looking for 40 acres.

We started making trips on the weekends when we could get away and we looked at a lot of different places. And one day this realtor that we had talked to said, "*I found a piece of property in the little town by Los Alamos. You might want to go and look at it even though it's bigger than what you want. It's two 100 hundred-acre parcels being sold together.* "

It was the spring of 1991 right after a rainy winter. In the spring, after the rainy season, the hills and fields are green and lush with growth. It was spectacular. We learned it is called being under the spell of the "green ether". Betty and I stood out in the middle of this green field and said to one another, "*Let's do this.*" I said, "*Well, why not one of the parcels?*" Betty said, "*Y*ou've got to buy them both.*" And* we did, and *i*t turned out to be an excellent decision. There was a windmill and land with enough length for a runway. Perfect!

In the beginning there wasn't much here: a road, water well, and a few fences. Had I understood the problems in the size of the project that I was getting ourselves into, I might not have gone through with it. I didn't understand anything about wells, water, electricity, roads, or fences. Betty and I had been in the city our whole lives and here we found ourselves in the country, and no understanding of what it takes to build fences, repair plows, tractors and the list goes on. It was and still is a great learning experience. (Our son and wife live here now and are learning this).

There were no houses on the property. We purchased a 20-foot trailer, and initially, what we did was park it underneath one of the trees and left it here. We would come on the weekends and stay in the trailer and had a wonderful time. Little by little, we started building. The first building, of course, was a barn. In the barn we added a shower and toilet. The next phase was a small house. I was still working full time and didn't have a lot of extra time to spend here. Then the business was sold and I found myself retired. We built a bigger house, sold our home in Rancho Palos Verdes and moved here permanently in 1997.

Early on, when I was probably 21 or 22, and we were living in Oxnard, I often drove by the airport in Oxnard called The Oxnard Civil Airport, and on the side of a big old hangar was a big sign that said, "*Learn to Fly.*" One day I stopped, walked in and I said, "*I'd like to have a flying lesson.*" The guy said "*OK.*" You get a flying lesson in an airplane with the instructor and the gasoline for $7 an hour.

I went out with a pilot/instructor named Floyd Jennings for my first flying lesson, and then went back for a second. One day after I had been flying with him for about six hours, he said, "*OK. Pullover to the side of the runway, and I'm getting out. You're going solo.*" And I said, *Are you sure?*" I went around the pattern, didn't crash, came back, and eventually, I got my license. So, this gets back to why we call the ranch *The Flying Z.*

When we started coming up here, we thought, well, we need to have a name for our ranch. And our last name being Ziegler, and me liking to fly airplanes, I thought, oh, what the heck? We'll call it The Flying Z Ranch. We were up here one weekend a guy came by with a big road grading machine. And I asked him:" *Can you grade a dirt strip in the middle of this field? I want to use it for landing and taking off in my airplane.*" And he says, "*Sure, I'll do that.*" He created a dirt runway for me and this runway is still there. I've since planted the runway with grass, so it's grass now, but it is still there, gophers included.

During this particular time, I had an airplane which was a Beech A36. It was a good airplane - fast and rugged. We could leave Torrance (where we used to live nearby in Rancho Palos Verdes) on a Friday night at 5 o'clock, when all the freeways were jammed with traffic. We could fly from Torrance to the ranch in about 40 minutes, and how we loved that! Otherwise, it would have been a mean, three and a half-hour drive through heavy, nasty traffic. We kept a car at the ranch so we could get around. Betty and I would fly up and land on the ranch runway we had put in. We'd go out to dinner or do whatever we wanted to do, and then on Sunday night, we'd turn around and fly back home. Our dog Junior loved to fly with us. He would go to sleep in the back and wake up when he heard the wheels go down.

It worked out well for several years until we were able to move permanently. So that was wonderful. As far as I am concerned, moving out of the city and here to the ranch was the best thing that I've ever done in my life. And the amount of knowledge I've gained by being on the ranch - so many things - just incredible- like water wells, electricity, tractors, crops, animals. The community we live in holds wonderful values and the people are nice. We help each other out.

Over the years, airplanes and I have gotten along really well. It's been a lot of fun. I like planes and flying. I wish I had done it earlier, and I wish I had done it more. We used to fly on longer trips. We went to *The Mexican Baja Peninsula*. We used to go there at least once a year, often down to Cabo San Lucas with stops at little places down the peninsula. We went down to the Mexican mainland and to Puerto Vallarta and Guadalajara.

When you fly to another country the correct registration is essential as is Insurance. First you stop at the nearest airport entering and then you are verified for correct information and you fill forms out. They need to know your destination. Upon returning you must land at the first American airport and basically repeat again. They want to know where you have been, etc. As I understand Mexican air traffic is much more difficult than when I was flying down there.

I still have an airplane here on the ranch, and my own little airport. I fly every ten days or so. The nice thing about this is that I can take the plane out, take off and fly around for an hour or twenty minutes, land, put the plane back in the barn/hangar, and then do something else for the rest of the day., I am fortunate.

Target (Best Dog Ever) in our Carbon Cab

Our Logo (Ron Designed)

Old Airstrip

Target in the Koi Pond

Betty's Birdhouse Grain Bin
Upside Down

Fall

Ranch Guard Geese

Waldo, the water buffalo

Field of Mustard

Ron's 2006 Dodge   *Flying Z Watusi*

Ron waiting to tell you his infamous stories.

My wife and I have had a happy and blessed life. And we feel thankful to have been able to move out of the city, and live here in this beautiful rural area. The lifestyle is wonderful, and we find the people much more friendly. The pace of life is slower, and we feel it is a better quality of life.

We are now both past eighty and still enjoying ourselves. We agree that when we were younger, we would never have thought that life would have been so good to us. In over sixty years of marriage the only bad years were when our son, Jeff, suffered a traumatic brain injury in a fall from a cliff. This was when he was 21. He passed away on September 29, 2004 at age 43.

While it is difficult to explain, certainly Jeff's injury and passing greatly changed our lives. We don't know what was to be, only what it has been and for that we are thankful.

Tim and Ron with Westco Container

Chapter Five
Life's Happenings

Tim's Wedding
Ron, Jeff, Tim & Betty

Ron Baking Bread

Ron and His Siblings

Tom, Ron, Judi, Douglas, Ken

Bhutan, Singapore

Ron Taming A Tiger

Bhutan

Singapore

Thailand

The Tiger is Tamed
Note it is a real tiger

Family Trips

Rachael, Tim, Betty, Tom, Megan, Ron (Taking Picture)

Megan, Tim, Tom, Rachael, Betty, Ron,

Ron, Rachael, Megan

Antartica
Boatload Going To Shore

On The Way To Adventure
Antartica

Clipper Adventurer Antartica
Mount Ziegler named after Ron's Historic Climb

South Georgia Island

Betty & Ron at Sir Earnest Shackleton Grave

Ron & Betty

World Famous Bar in Stanleyville, Falkland Island.

Ron & Betty

Ron & Betty

Ron, Betty & Megan

Ron & Doug

Betty & Ron

Tim & Ron - England

Ken & Ron

Ron & Red Rock Fish

Alaska

Ron Hugging A Salmon

Ron in Alaska

Ron

Ron & Betty

Ron Training Bulls

Hawaii

Sitell Beach
Sunset
Favorite Time Of Day

The Ultimate Workbook
for Preserving Your Legacy & You

Write Heart Memories®
Beth Lord

Available on www.bethlord.com &
www.amazon.com
Online Support Step by Step
The Easy Way To Get Your Stories In A Book.

Write Heart Memories®

Made in the USA
Middletown, DE
07 June 2021